Quantum Computing Demystified

Unlocking the Future of Technology

By Oluchi Ike

Preface

The future is quantum. As we stand on the brink of a technological revolution, quantum computing emerges as a field that has the potential to redefine our understanding of computation, problem-solving, and innovation. This book, *Quantum Computing Demystified: Unlocking the Future of Technology*, aims to bridge the gap between the complexities of quantum mechanics and the practical possibilities of quantum computing, making it accessible to both beginners and seasoned tech enthusiasts.

Quantum computing is often perceived as an intimidating and highly theoretical subject, reserved for physicists and mathematicians. However, as advancements in this field accelerate, the need for a broader understanding becomes essential. This book is crafted with the intent of simplifying the intricate world of qubits, superposition, and entanglement, presenting these concepts in an approachable manner. Through real-world examples, analogies, and clear explanations, we aim to make quantum computing not just understandable but exciting.

Whether you're a student exploring cutting-edge technologies, a professional looking to expand your skills, or simply curious about the future of computing, this book is your guide to the quantum realm. From foundational principles to programming and real-world applications, you'll discover how quantum computing is not just a theoretical pursuit but a transformative force shaping industries and society. Welcome to a journey into the quantum frontier.

Table of Contents

Preface

Chapter 1: Introduction to Quantum Computing

1.1 What Is Quantum Computing?

1.2 How It Differs from Classical Computing

1.3 A Brief History of Quantum Computing

Chapter 2: The Foundations of Quantum Mechanics

2.1 Qubits: The Building Blocks of Quantum Computing

2.2 Superposition and Entanglement Explained

2.3 Quantum Gates and Circuits

Chapter 3: Building Quantum Computers

3.1 The Science Behind Quantum Hardware

3.2 Types of Quantum Computers: Superconducting Qubits, Trapped Ions, and Beyond

3.3 Challenges in Quantum Hardware Development

Chapter 4: Programming Quantum Computers

4.1 Introduction to Quantum Programming Languages (Qiskit, Cirq, etc.)

4.2 Writing and Running Your First Quantum Program

4.3 Debugging and Testing Quantum Code

Chapter 5: Quantum Algorithms

5.1 Shor's Algorithm: Breaking Cryptography

5.2 Grover's Algorithm: Quantum Search

5.3 Emerging Algorithms and Their Applications

Chapter 6: Applications of Quantum Computing

6.1 Quantum Computing in Cryptography

6.2 Drug Discovery and Material Science

6.3 Artificial Intelligence and Machine Learning

Chapter 7: Current Progress and Industry Leaders

7.1 Milestones in Quantum Computing

7.2 Key Players: IBM, Google, Microsoft, and Startups

7.3 The Roadmap to Quantum Supremacy

Chapter 8: Challenges and Ethical Considerations

8.1 Risks to Data Security and Privacy

8.2 Societal Impacts of Quantum Technologies

8.3 Ethical Questions in Quantum Computing

Chapter 9: The Future of Quantum Computing

9.1 Predictions for the Next Two Decades

9.2 Integration of Quantum and Classical Computing

9.3 Quantum Computing's Role in Global Challenges

Glossary of Quantum Computing Terms

Further Resources

Recommended Books

Online Courses and Tutorials

Quantum Computing Communities

References

Author's Note

This structure offers readers a logical progression from understanding the basics to exploring advanced concepts and practical applications, ensuring a comprehensive and engaging learning experience.

Chapter 1: Introduction to Quantum Computing

Quantum computing is not just the next step in the evolution of computing; it represents an entirely new paradigm. This chapter introduces the foundational concepts of quantum computing, highlights its key distinctions from classical computing, and explores its fascinating history, setting the stage for understanding this transformative technology.

1.1 What Is Quantum Computing?

At its core, quantum computing leverages the principles of quantum mechanics—the branch of physics that deals with the behavior of particles at microscopic scales—to perform computations. Unlike classical computers, which process information using binary bits (0s and 1s), quantum computers use **quantum bits**, or **qubits**. A qubit can represent both 0 and 1 simultaneously, thanks to a property called **superposition**.

This unique characteristic allows quantum computers to perform many calculations simultaneously, making them exponentially faster at solving certain problems compared to classical computers. For example, while a classical computer might methodically test every possible solution to a problem one at a time, a quantum computer can explore multiple solutions at once.

Another fundamental property of quantum computing is **entanglement**. When two qubits become entangled, the state of one qubit is instantly correlated with the state of the other, regardless of the physical distance between them. This phenomenon allows quantum computers to perform highly complex calculations through interconnected qubits.

Quantum computing is particularly suited for problems involving massive amounts of data or scenarios where multiple variables need to be analyzed simultaneously. Applications range from breaking cryptographic codes and optimizing supply chains to revolutionizing drug discovery and artificial intelligence.

1.2 How It Differs from Classical Computing

To appreciate the significance of quantum computing, it's essential to understand how it differs from classical computing. Classical computers, including the ones we use daily, rely on **binary logic**, where every piece of data is represented as either a 0 or a 1. These bits are processed by a series of logic gates, which perform specific operations to solve problems.

Quantum computers, by contrast, rely on **quantum bits** that can exist in multiple states simultaneously due to superposition. This means a quantum computer with just a few qubits can represent an astronomical number of states at once, unlike a classical computer, which would require an exponentially larger number of bits.

For example, if a classical computer has nnn bits, it can represent $2n2^{\wedge}n2n$ possible states, but only one state at a time. In contrast, a quantum computer with nnn qubits can represent and process all $2n2^{\wedge}n2n$ states simultaneously. This parallelism enables quantum computers to solve specific types of problems much faster than classical computers.

Another key difference lies in the concept of **quantum gates**, which operate on qubits. Unlike classical gates (AND, OR, NOT, etc.), quantum gates manipulate qubits using principles like superposition and entanglement. These gates perform complex operations that are central to quantum algorithms, enabling computations that classical computers cannot efficiently replicate.

Despite these advantages, quantum computers are not universally superior to classical computers. They excel at solving specific problems, such as factoring large numbers or simulating quantum systems, but they are not designed to replace classical computers for everyday tasks like word processing or browsing the internet. Instead, quantum computers are seen as complementary to classical systems, tackling problems that classical computers cannot efficiently solve.

1.3 A Brief History of Quantum Computing

The journey of quantum computing began in the 20th century with the development of quantum mechanics, a field of physics that fundamentally challenged classical theories. Here is a timeline of significant milestones that shaped the evolution of quantum computing:

Theoretical Foundations (1900–1970s)

- **1900s:** The roots of quantum mechanics were established by physicists like Max Planck and Albert Einstein, who introduced groundbreaking ideas about the behavior of particles and energy at microscopic scales.

- **1920s–1930s:** Pioneers like Erwin Schrödinger, Werner Heisenberg, and Niels Bohr formalized the principles of quantum mechanics, including superposition and entanglement, laying the groundwork for future technological applications.

- **1970s:** Physicist Richard Feynman first proposed the idea of a quantum computer. He suggested that quantum systems could be simulated more effectively using quantum mechanics rather than classical computation, sparking interest in the potential of quantum computing.

Early Development (1980s–1990s)

- **1981:** At a conference at MIT, Richard Feynman articulated his vision of a quantum computer that could simulate quantum phenomena. This idea inspired researchers to explore how quantum mechanics could be applied to computation.

- **1985:** David Deutsch, a physicist at the University of Oxford, developed the concept of a universal quantum computer. He also proposed the first quantum algorithm, demonstrating that quantum systems could solve certain problems more efficiently than classical ones.

- **1994:** Peter Shor, a mathematician, introduced Shor's algorithm, a breakthrough that showed quantum computers could factorize large numbers exponentially faster than classical computers. This discovery had profound implications for cryptography and spurred significant interest in quantum computing.

Modern Advances (2000s–Present)

- **2001:** IBM and Stanford University successfully implemented Shor's algorithm on a quantum computer for the first time, marking a major milestone in practical quantum computing.

- **2011:** D-Wave Systems, a Canadian company, launched the first commercially available quantum computer. Although it was a specialized system (quantum annealer) and not a general-purpose quantum computer, it demonstrated that quantum computing technology could be commercialized.

- **2019:** Google achieved a milestone in quantum computing by claiming "quantum supremacy." Using its Sycamore quantum processor, Google solved a problem in 200 seconds that would take the most powerful classical supercomputer thousands of years.

- **2020s:** Quantum computing continues to advance, with major companies like IBM, Google, and Microsoft competing to develop more stable and scalable quantum systems. Startups and academic institutions worldwide are contributing to this rapidly evolving field.

The Road Ahead

While quantum computing is still in its infancy, its potential is enormous. Researchers are actively working on improving the stability of qubits, scaling up quantum processors, and developing new quantum algorithms. Governments and private organizations are investing heavily in quantum research, recognizing its transformative potential in areas like cybersecurity, healthcare, and artificial intelligence.

Conclusion

Quantum computing represents a radical departure from traditional computing paradigms. By leveraging the principles of quantum mechanics, it offers the potential to solve problems that are currently intractable for classical computers. This chapter has introduced the foundational concepts of quantum computing, explained its key differences from classical systems, and provided an overview of its fascinating history. As we delve deeper into this field, we will explore the science, programming, and applications that make quantum computing one of the most exciting technological frontiers of our time.

Chapter 2: The Foundations of Quantum Mechanics

Quantum computing rests on the profound principles of quantum mechanics, the physics governing the microscopic world of atoms and particles. To understand quantum computing, one must first grasp the underlying concepts that make it possible. This chapter delves into the foundational elements of quantum mechanics as applied to computing, including qubits, the phenomena of superposition and entanglement, and the role of quantum gates and circuits in executing computations.

2.1 Qubits: The Building Blocks of Quantum Computing

In classical computing, information is represented as binary bits, taking the value of either 0 or 1. Quantum computing, however, uses quantum bits or **qubits**, which represent the fundamental units of information in a quantum system.

Physical Realizations of Qubits

Qubits are typically represented by quantum systems such as electrons, photons, or atomic nuclei. These systems have measurable states, such as the spin of an electron or the polarization of a photon, which can represent 0, 1, or a combination of both. For instance:

- **Electron spin:** A spin-up state might represent 0, while a spin-down state represents 1.

- **Photon polarization:** Vertical polarization could denote 0, and horizontal polarization could represent 1.

Quantum States and Bloch Sphere Representation

Unlike classical bits, qubits can exist in a **quantum state**, which is a superposition of 0 and 1. Mathematically, a quantum state is represented as:

$$|\psi\rangle = \alpha|0\rangle + \beta|1\rangle$$

where α and β are complex numbers that denote the probability amplitudes of the qubit being in states $|0\rangle$ and $|1\rangle$, respectively. The probabilities must satisfy the condition:

$$|\alpha|^2 + |\beta|^2 = 1$$

A common way to visualize a qubit's state is through the **Bloch sphere**, a 3D representation of all possible quantum states. The north and south poles correspond to the classical states $|0\rangle$ and $|1\rangle$, while any point on the sphere represents a superposition state.

Key Properties of Qubits

- **Superposition:** A qubit can exist in a combination of states 0 and 1 until measured.
- **Entanglement:** Qubits can become correlated in ways that their individual states depend on each other, even across distances.
- **Decoherence:** Qubits are extremely sensitive to their environment, and their quantum state can collapse or degrade, a challenge for quantum computing.

Qubits serve as the foundation for quantum computations, enabling the vast computational power that distinguishes quantum systems from classical systems.

2.2 Superposition and Entanglement Explained

Two phenomena central to the power of quantum computing are **superposition** and **entanglement**. These principles differentiate quantum systems from classical systems and allow for exponential computational gains.

Superposition

Superposition is the property of a qubit to exist simultaneously in a combination of states. In a classical system, a bit is definitively either 0 or 1, but in a quantum system, a qubit exists as a mixture of these states until measured.

For example, a single qubit in superposition can be in the state:

$$|\psi\rangle = \frac{1}{\sqrt{2}}|0\rangle + \frac{1}{\sqrt{2}}|1\rangle$$

This state means the qubit has an equal probability of collapsing to 0 or 1 when measured. Superposition enables quantum computers to process multiple possibilities simultaneously, dramatically increasing their computational capacity.

Entanglement

Entanglement is a phenomenon in which the states of two or more qubits become interdependent. When qubits are entangled, the state of one qubit cannot be described independently of the other, regardless of the physical distance between them.

For example, consider two qubits in an entangled state:

$$|\psi\rangle = \frac{1}{\sqrt{2}}|00\rangle + \frac{1}{\sqrt{2}}|11\rangle$$

If one qubit is measured and found to be in state $|0\rangle$, the other qubit will immediately be in state $|0\rangle$ as well, and vice versa for $|1\rangle$. This correlation persists even if the qubits are separated by large distances.

Entanglement plays a critical role in quantum computing by enabling quantum error correction, secure communication, and the parallel processing of information. However, achieving and maintaining entanglement is technically challenging due to environmental interference.

2.3 Quantum Gates and Circuits

Quantum gates and circuits form the operational framework of quantum computers, enabling them to perform computations.

Quantum Gates

Quantum gates manipulate qubits, altering their states through specific quantum operations. Unlike classical logic gates, which process bits, quantum gates operate on qubits using principles of quantum mechanics.

Some common quantum gates include:

1. **Pauli-X Gate (NOT Gate):** Flips the state of a qubit. If the input is $|0\rangle$, the output is $|1\rangle$, and vice versa.

$$X|0\rangle = |1\rangle, \quad X|1\rangle = |0\rangle$$

2. **Hadamard Gate (H):** Creates superposition by transforming a qubit from a definite state into a combination of states.

$$H|0\rangle = \frac{1}{\sqrt{2}}(|0\rangle + |1\rangle)$$

3. **CNOT Gate (Controlled NOT):** Operates on two qubits and flips the second qubit (target) if the first qubit (control) is in state $|1\rangle$.

4. **Phase Gates (S, T):** Apply phase shifts to qubits, altering the relative phase between quantum states.

Quantum gates are represented as matrices, and their operations are applied to qubit states through matrix multiplication. These gates are reversible, meaning information is never lost—a key feature of quantum mechanics.

Quantum Circuits

Quantum circuits are sequences of quantum gates applied to qubits to perform specific computations. A circuit consists of:

- **Qubits:** The information carriers.
- **Quantum Gates:** Operations that manipulate qubits.
- **Measurement:** The process of collapsing qubits into classical bits at the end of the computation.

A simple quantum circuit might involve:

1. Initializing a qubit to $|0\rangle$ |0\rangle|0⟩.
2. Applying a Hadamard gate to create superposition.
3. Using a CNOT gate to entangle the qubit with another.
4. Measuring the qubits to extract a result.

Quantum circuits are typically visualized as diagrams, with horizontal lines representing qubits and boxes indicating gates. The complexity of a circuit depends on the problem being solved, with more intricate problems requiring larger circuits and more qubits.

Quantum Algorithms and Quantum Advantage

Quantum gates and circuits enable the implementation of quantum algorithms, which solve problems more efficiently than classical algorithms. Examples include:

- **Shor's Algorithm:** Efficiently factors large numbers, breaking certain cryptographic codes.
- **Grover's Algorithm:** Accelerates unstructured search problems.

The goal of quantum computing is to achieve **quantum advantage**, where a quantum computer outperforms the best classical computer on a specific task.

Conclusion

The principles of quantum mechanics—qubits, superposition, and entanglement—form the bedrock of quantum computing, offering unparalleled computational power. By harnessing these properties through quantum gates and circuits, quantum computers can perform complex operations that are infeasible for classical computers. As we explore more about this transformative technology, the fundamental understanding of these components will provide a solid foundation for comprehending advanced concepts and applications.

Chapter 3: Building Quantum Computers

The realization of quantum computing is as much an engineering challenge as it is a scientific revolution. Unlike classical computers, which rely on well-established silicon-based technology, quantum computers leverage the principles of quantum mechanics to perform computations. This chapter explores the science behind quantum hardware, examines different types of quantum computers, and highlights the challenges involved in developing quantum systems that are scalable, reliable, and practical.

3.1 The Science Behind Quantum Hardware

Quantum hardware is built upon the principles of quantum mechanics, particularly leveraging the phenomena of **superposition**, **entanglement**, and **quantum tunneling**. Designing hardware to harness these principles requires manipulating quantum particles under highly controlled conditions.

Quantum State Initialization

The first step in building a quantum computer involves initializing qubits into a known state, typically $|0\rangle$|0\rangle|0⟩. Achieving this requires sophisticated techniques depending on the physical realization of the qubits, such as cooling superconducting materials to near absolute zero or using lasers to manipulate ions.

Quantum State Control

Precise control over quantum states is vital for quantum computation. Quantum operations are implemented using external fields like magnetic fields, radiofrequency waves, or laser pulses. This precision ensures that quantum gates can accurately manipulate qubits to perform desired operations.

Quantum Measurement

At the end of a quantum computation, qubits are measured to extract classical information. Measurement collapses the quantum state into a definite value, either 0 or 1. Designing hardware for accurate and non-destructive measurements is a critical aspect of quantum hardware development.

Error Correction and Decoherence Mitigation

Quantum systems are inherently fragile and susceptible to **decoherence**, where qubits lose their quantum state due to interactions with the environment. Advanced error correction techniques, such as redundancy using multiple physical qubits to encode a single logical qubit, are employed to mitigate these issues.

Quantum hardware thus relies on a delicate balance of physics, materials science, and engineering to create and sustain the quantum states necessary for computation.

3.2 Types of Quantum Computers: Superconducting Qubits, Trapped Ions, and Beyond

Several approaches to building quantum computers have emerged, each with its unique advantages and challenges. These approaches are based on different physical systems used to implement qubits and perform quantum operations.

Superconducting Qubits

Superconducting qubits are one of the most mature and widely adopted technologies in quantum computing, utilized by companies like IBM, Google, and Rigetti.

- **How It Works:** Superconducting circuits, made from materials like aluminum or niobium, exhibit quantum behavior when cooled to near absolute zero. These circuits use Josephson junctions to create and control qubits.

- **Advantages:**
  - Fast gate operations, suitable for high-speed computations.
  - Strong support from industrial and academic research communities.

- **Challenges:**
  - Requires ultra-low temperatures, maintained by expensive cryogenic systems.
  - Susceptible to decoherence, with short coherence times.

Trapped Ions

Trapped ion quantum computers manipulate individual ions (charged atoms) as qubits using electromagnetic fields. Companies like IonQ and Honeywell are pioneering this approach.

- **How It Works:**
  - Ions are trapped in electromagnetic fields and manipulated using laser pulses to perform quantum operations.
  - Entanglement is achieved through shared vibrational modes of the ions.

- **Advantages:**
  - Long coherence times, enabling more reliable computations.
  - High precision in gate operations.

- **Challenges:**

- Slower gate speeds compared to superconducting qubits.
- Scalability is limited by the complexity of managing large ion arrays.

Photonic Quantum Computers

Photonic quantum computers use photons as qubits, encoding information in properties such as polarization or phase.

- **How It Works:**
  - Light sources, waveguides, and detectors are used to create and manipulate photonic qubits.
  - Interference and measurement techniques are applied for computation.
- **Advantages:**
  - Operates at room temperature, reducing cooling requirements.
  - Potential for integration with existing optical communication technologies.
- **Challenges:**
  - Difficulty in achieving reliable entanglement and gate operations.
  - High losses during photon transmission and detection.

Other Emerging Approaches

- **Topological Quantum Computers:** Use anyons, exotic particles predicted by quantum field theory, to encode qubits in a way that is inherently error-resistant.

- **Quantum Annealers:** Designed specifically for optimization problems, as seen in D-Wave's machines, but less general-purpose compared to gate-based quantum computers.

- **Neutral Atom Quantum Computers:** Use neutral atoms manipulated by optical tweezers, offering potential scalability advantages.

Each type of quantum computer represents a trade-off between speed, reliability, scalability, and complexity. The race to build the most effective quantum computer involves exploring and refining these diverse approaches.

3.3 Challenges in Quantum Hardware Development

The development of quantum computers faces numerous technical and practical challenges, many of which stem from the delicate nature of quantum systems and the nascent state of the field.

1. Maintaining Quantum Coherence

One of the most significant challenges in quantum hardware development is maintaining quantum coherence. Qubits are highly sensitive to external disturbances, such as vibrations, temperature fluctuations, and electromagnetic noise. These disturbances cause decoherence, which limits the time available for computations.

To address this:

- Superconducting qubits require cryogenic systems to operate at millikelvin temperatures.

- Error correction techniques, such as surface codes and stabilizer codes, are used to protect quantum information.

2. Scaling Up Qubit Numbers

For quantum computers to solve meaningful problems, they need thousands or even millions of qubits. Scaling up qubit numbers while maintaining control and coherence is a daunting challenge.

- Physical systems like trapped ions and superconducting qubits require complex infrastructure that grows exponentially with qubit count.
- Advances in fabrication techniques and modular architectures are being explored to enable scalability.

3. Error Rates and Fault Tolerance

Quantum gates and measurements are prone to errors, which accumulate as computations progress. Achieving fault-tolerant quantum computing requires error rates below a critical threshold and robust error correction protocols. Current hardware struggles to meet these requirements.

4. Interconnects and Communication

As quantum computers grow larger, connecting qubits across different parts of the system becomes a challenge. Quantum interconnects using photons or other mechanisms are being developed to address this issue.

5. Cost and Accessibility

Quantum hardware development is resource-intensive, involving advanced materials, precision instruments, and cryogenic systems. This restricts access to quantum computers to a small number of organizations, slowing broader innovation. Efforts to make quantum computing more accessible, such as cloud-based platforms, are emerging to democratize the technology.

6. Environmental Control

Quantum systems must operate in highly controlled environments to prevent external noise from disrupting computations. Maintaining such environments is technically and financially demanding, especially for technologies like superconducting qubits.

7. Integration with Classical Systems

Quantum computers require seamless integration with classical systems for input/output operations, error correction, and algorithm execution. Developing efficient hybrid systems is a key area of ongoing research.

8. Uncertain Applications and Use Cases

While quantum computing promises breakthroughs in fields like cryptography, materials science, and optimization, identifying practical, near-term applications remains a challenge. This uncertainty makes it difficult to prioritize hardware development efforts.

Conclusion

Building quantum computers is a monumental endeavor that requires a deep understanding of quantum mechanics, materials science, and engineering. From superconducting qubits to trapped ions and photonic systems, each approach offers unique possibilities and faces distinct challenges. Overcoming the technical hurdles of coherence, scalability, and fault tolerance will be critical to unlocking the transformative potential of quantum computing. As the field continues to evolve, advancements in quantum hardware will pave the way for revolutionary applications that could redefine technology and society.

Chapter 4: Programming Quantum Computers

Programming a quantum computer is a fascinating journey into a new computational paradigm. Unlike classical programming, where binary logic dominates, quantum programming leverages the principles of quantum mechanics to perform computations. This chapter introduces popular quantum programming languages, guides you through writing and running your first quantum program, and explains the nuances of debugging and testing quantum code.

4.1 Introduction to Quantum Programming Languages (Qiskit, Cirq, etc.)

Quantum programming languages and frameworks serve as the bridge between high-level algorithms and the physical hardware of quantum computers. These tools provide developers with the means to design, simulate, and execute quantum programs without delving into the intricacies of hardware.

Popular Quantum Programming Languages

1. **Qiskit (IBM):**
   Qiskit, developed by IBM, is an open-source quantum computing framework.
   - **Features:**
     - Python-based, making it accessible to a wide audience.
     - Supports quantum circuit design, optimization, and execution on IBM Quantum hardware.
     - Includes modules like Qiskit Terra (circuit design), Qiskit Aer (simulation), and Qiskit Ignis (error mitigation).

- **Strengths:**
    - Large community and extensive documentation.
    - Access to IBM's real quantum computers through the IBM Quantum Experience platform.

2. **Cirq (Google):**

Cirq, developed by Google, is another Python-based framework tailored for research and development.

- **Features:**
    - Focuses on low-level circuit design and optimization.
    - Provides tools for creating, simulating, and executing quantum circuits on Google's Sycamore hardware.
- **Strengths:**
    - Designed with hardware compatibility in mind, making it ideal for advanced quantum experiments.

3. **PennyLane:**

PennyLane combines quantum computing and machine learning, offering tools for hybrid quantum-classical computations.

- **Features:**
    - Focus on variational quantum algorithms.
    - Integrates with machine learning libraries like TensorFlow and PyTorch.

4. **QuTiP (Quantum Toolbox in Python):**

   QuTiP is primarily used for quantum mechanics simulations and is well-suited for educational purposes.

5. **Microsoft Quantum Development Kit (QDK) and Q#:**

   Microsoft's QDK includes Q#, a domain-specific language for quantum programming.

   - **Features:**
     - Integration with Visual Studio.
     - A focus on quantum algorithm development and simulations.

Selecting the Right Language

The choice of quantum programming language depends on your goals:

- Beginners and hobbyists might start with Qiskit for its user-friendly documentation.
- Researchers focusing on hardware might prefer Cirq or Q#.
- Machine learning enthusiasts can explore PennyLane.

4.2 Writing and Running Your First Quantum Program

Getting started with quantum programming involves setting up your environment, writing a basic quantum circuit, and executing it either on a simulator or real hardware.

Setting Up Your Environment

Before writing quantum programs, you need to install the necessary tools:

- For Qiskit: Install Python and use pip install qiskit.
- For Cirq: Install Python and use pip install cirq.
- Ensure you have an account with a quantum platform provider like IBM Quantum or Google Quantum AI for hardware access.

Understanding the Basics

Quantum programs are constructed as **quantum circuits**, which are sequences of operations (quantum gates) applied to qubits.

Example: Creating a Simple Quantum Circuit

Below is an example of a simple Qiskit program:

python

Copy code

```
from qiskit import QuantumCircuit, Aer, execute

# Step 1: Create a quantum circuit with one qubit and one classical bit
qc = QuantumCircuit(1, 1)

# Step 2: Apply a Hadamard gate to the qubit (puts it in superposition)
qc.h(0)

# Step 3: Measure the qubit
qc.measure(0, 0)
```

Step 4: Simulate the circuit

simulator = Aer.get_backend('qasm_simulator')

result = execute(qc, simulator).result()

counts = result.get_counts()

Step 5: Print the result

print("Measurement results:", counts)

Explanation:

- A **Hadamard gate** creates a superposition of $|0\rangle$ |0\rangle|0) and $|1\rangle$ |1\rangle|1).

- The **measurement** collapses the superposition into a classical state (0 or 1).

- The program simulates the circuit using a quantum simulator.

Executing the Program on Real Hardware

Executing a quantum program on actual hardware follows a similar workflow, but you'll need access to a quantum computer:

1. Connect to the provider's API (e.g., IBM Quantum).

2. Submit your quantum circuit.

3. Wait for the job to be processed (quantum computers often have queues).

4.3 Debugging and Testing Quantum Code

Debugging quantum programs is fundamentally different from classical debugging due to the probabilistic nature of quantum mechanics. Unlike classical programs, where outputs are deterministic, quantum programs often produce probabilistic results, making debugging a nuanced process.

Challenges in Debugging Quantum Code

1. **Probabilistic Outputs:**
    - The same quantum program can produce different results on multiple runs due to the inherent uncertainty of quantum measurements.

2. **State Collapse:**
    - Measuring a quantum state during debugging destroys the state, preventing further computation.

3. **Hardware Errors:**
    - Noise and decoherence in quantum hardware introduce errors that are hard to isolate and debug.

Strategies for Debugging Quantum Programs

1. Use Simulators:
Simulators are essential tools for testing quantum circuits without the limitations of real hardware. They allow you to:

- Visualize quantum states at each step.
- Analyze errors in circuit design.

2. Validate Small Circuits:
Break down large circuits into smaller, testable components. Validate each component individually to ensure correctness.

3. Analyze Output Probabilities:

Quantum programs often produce probability distributions as outputs. Compare these distributions with expected results to identify discrepancies.

4. Leverage Tools and Libraries:

Quantum programming frameworks provide built-in tools for debugging.

- Qiskit includes the **qiskit.visualization** module for circuit and state visualization.

- Cirq offers state simulators to inspect intermediate quantum states.

5. Incorporate Error Mitigation Techniques:

Noise and errors in quantum hardware can affect results. Implement error mitigation strategies such as:

- Running circuits multiple times and averaging results.

- Using error correction codes.

6. Monitor Resource Usage:

Quantum algorithms can become computationally expensive on real hardware. Use resource estimation tools to optimize qubit usage and gate counts.

Debugging Example:

Suppose a quantum program unexpectedly produces a 50/50 output distribution when a deterministic result is expected. The issue might stem from:

- An unintentional gate operation (e.g., a missing NOT gate).

- Incorrect qubit initialization.

By simulating the circuit and analyzing intermediate states, you can pinpoint the error and correct it.

Conclusion

Programming quantum computers is a blend of creativity, logic, and an understanding of quantum mechanics. From exploring programming languages like Qiskit and Cirq to writing and debugging quantum programs, the field offers exciting opportunities to solve problems in novel ways. While challenges like probabilistic outputs and hardware noise make quantum programming complex, advances in tooling and resources are steadily lowering the barriers to entry. As you continue your journey into quantum programming, mastering these tools and techniques will empower you to unlock the full potential of quantum computing.

Chapter 5: Quantum Algorithms

Quantum algorithms represent the cutting edge of computational science, offering the potential to solve certain problems exponentially faster than classical algorithms. They exploit the principles of quantum mechanics, such as superposition and entanglement, to process information in ways that are impossible for classical computers. This chapter delves into some of the most significant quantum algorithms: Shor's algorithm for breaking cryptographic systems, Grover's algorithm for quantum search, and emerging algorithms that are shaping the future of quantum computing applications.

5.1 Shor's Algorithm: Breaking Cryptography

Shor's algorithm, developed by mathematician Peter Shor in 1994, is one of the most famous quantum algorithms. Its ability to factor large integers efficiently threatens the security of widely used cryptographic systems, particularly those based on RSA encryption.

The Problem with Classical Factoring

RSA encryption relies on the difficulty of factoring large numbers into their prime components. Classical computers struggle with this task, as the time required grows exponentially with the size of the number. This computational difficulty forms the backbone of RSA's security.

How Shor's Algorithm Works

Shor's algorithm transforms the factoring problem into a periodicity problem, which quantum computers excel at solving. Here's a simplified overview:

1. **Reduction to Modular Arithmetic:**

   The algorithm reduces the factoring problem to finding the period of a function related to modular exponentiation.

2. **Quantum Fourier Transform (QFT):**

   The algorithm uses the QFT, a quantum analog of the discrete Fourier transform, to identify the period of the function.

3. **Classical Post-Processing:**

   Once the period is determined, classical computations complete the factorization process.

Impact on Cryptography

If large-scale quantum computers become operational, Shor's algorithm could render RSA and similar encryption systems obsolete. This has spurred research into quantum-resistant cryptographic methods, such as lattice-based and hash-based encryption.

5.2 Grover's Algorithm: Quantum Search

Grover's algorithm, proposed by Lov Grover in 1996, is a quantum search algorithm that provides a quadratic speedup for unstructured search problems.

The Problem with Classical Search

Classical search algorithms, such as linear search, require $O(N)O(N)O(N)$ time to find a specific item in an unsorted database of NNN items. This becomes computationally expensive for large datasets.

How Grover's Algorithm Works

Grover's algorithm leverages quantum superposition and interference to locate the target item in $O(\sqrt{N})$ steps.

1. **Initialization:**

   The algorithm starts by creating a superposition of all possible states in the database, assigning equal probability amplitudes to each.

2. **Oracle Query:**

   A quantum oracle identifies the target state by flipping its phase.

3. **Amplitude Amplification:**

   Using the Grover diffusion operator, the algorithm amplifies the probability of the target state while reducing the probabilities of all others.

4. **Measurement:**

   After a sufficient number of iterations, measuring the quantum state collapses it to the target state with high probability.

Applications of Grover's Algorithm

- **Database Search:** Grover's algorithm is useful for searching unsorted databases and datasets.

- **Optimization Problems:** It can be applied to combinatorial optimization problems by encoding them as search problems.

- **Cryptographic Analysis:** Grover's algorithm can speed up brute-force attacks on symmetric-key cryptography, reducing the complexity from $O(2^n)$ to $O(2^{n/2})$.

Limitations

Grover's algorithm does not achieve exponential speedup like Shor's algorithm and is limited to quadratic improvements. However, this speedup is still significant for large-scale problems.

5.3 Emerging Algorithms and Their Applications

Beyond Shor's and Grover's algorithms, a growing array of quantum algorithms promises to revolutionize various fields, from material science to machine learning.

Variational Quantum Algorithms (VQAs)

Variational quantum algorithms are designed to leverage the current capabilities of quantum hardware, which are limited by noise and scalability.

- **Variational Quantum Eigensolver (VQE):**
  VQE approximates the ground-state energy of a quantum system, making it valuable for studying molecular chemistry and material properties.

- **Quantum Approximate Optimization Algorithm (QAOA):**
  QAOA solves combinatorial optimization problems by combining classical and quantum computations. Applications include logistics, scheduling, and portfolio optimization.

Quantum Machine Learning (QML)

Quantum machine learning aims to accelerate machine learning tasks by exploiting quantum principles.

- **Quantum Support Vector Machines (QSVM):**
  QSVMs improve classification tasks by utilizing quantum feature spaces.

- **Quantum Neural Networks (QNN):**

    Quantum versions of neural networks hold potential for pattern recognition and image analysis.

Quantum Simulation Algorithms

Quantum simulation algorithms excel at modeling complex quantum systems that are intractable for classical computers.

- **Applications in Chemistry:**

    Quantum simulations enable precise modeling of molecular interactions, aiding drug discovery and materials design.

- **Applications in Physics:**

    These algorithms help simulate quantum phenomena, such as high-temperature superconductivity.

Quantum Cryptographic Algorithms

Quantum cryptography provides secure communication methods resistant to both classical and quantum attacks.

- **Quantum Key Distribution (QKD):**

    Protocols like BB84 enable secure key exchange using quantum mechanics.

- **Post-Quantum Cryptography:**

    Research is ongoing into classical cryptographic methods resistant to quantum attacks.

Quantum Annealing Algorithms

Quantum annealing, implemented in systems like D-Wave, tackles optimization problems by exploiting quantum tunneling.

- **Applications in AI:**

    Quantum annealers optimize machine learning models.

- **Applications in Finance:**

    They help optimize investment portfolios and risk management strategies.

Limitations and Future Directions

While emerging algorithms are promising, their practical applications are currently constrained by hardware limitations, noise, and scalability challenges. As quantum hardware improves, the range and impact of these algorithms are expected to expand dramatically.

Conclusion

Quantum algorithms are transforming the landscape of computational science, offering solutions to problems previously deemed intractable. Shor's algorithm demonstrates the disruptive potential of quantum computing in cryptography, while Grover's algorithm provides significant speedups in search and optimization tasks. Emerging algorithms, including variational methods and quantum simulations, hint at a future where quantum computing drives advancements in fields like chemistry, machine learning, and optimization.

As quantum technology continues to evolve, so too will the development of algorithms tailored to exploit its unique capabilities. Understanding these algorithms is crucial not only for researchers and developers but also for industries poised to harness the transformative power of quantum computing. The algorithms presented in this chapter are just the beginning of what promises to be a revolution in computation and problem-solving.

Chapter 6: Applications of Quantum Computing

Quantum computing, with its immense computational power and novel problem-solving approaches, is poised to revolutionize various industries. By harnessing the principles of quantum mechanics, quantum computers can tackle challenges that are intractable for classical computers. This chapter explores three major domains where quantum computing is making significant strides: cryptography, drug discovery and material science, and artificial intelligence (AI) and machine learning (ML).

6.1 Quantum Computing in Cryptography

Cryptography has long been a cornerstone of secure communication in the digital age, and quantum computing is reshaping this field in profound ways.

Breaking Classical Cryptography

Many classical cryptographic systems, such as RSA and Diffie-Hellman, rely on the computational difficulty of problems like integer factorization and discrete logarithms. These problems are infeasible for classical computers to solve within a reasonable timeframe, providing the basis for secure encryption.

Quantum computers, however, can disrupt this security paradigm. Algorithms like Shor's algorithm can efficiently factorize large integers and compute discrete logarithms, rendering classical encryption schemes vulnerable. A quantum computer with enough qubits and stability could potentially break these encryption methods, exposing sensitive data.

Quantum-Resistant Cryptography

To counteract this threat, researchers are developing quantum-resistant cryptographic systems. These systems rely on problems that remain difficult for both classical and quantum computers, such as lattice-based, hash-based, and multivariate polynomial cryptography. The U.S. National Institute of Standards and Technology (NIST) is actively working to standardize quantum-resistant algorithms.

Quantum Key Distribution (QKD)

While quantum computers threaten existing cryptographic methods, they also offer new tools for secure communication. Quantum key distribution (QKD) uses the principles of quantum mechanics to securely exchange encryption keys. Protocols like BB84 ensure that any eavesdropping attempt alters the quantum state, alerting parties to the intrusion.

Applications of QKD include:

- **Secure Banking and Financial Transactions:** Protecting sensitive financial data.

- **Government and Military Communication:** Ensuring secure transmission of classified information.

- **Healthcare Data Protection:** Safeguarding patient records and medical research.

Challenges in Cryptographic Applications

Although QKD promises unbreakable encryption, practical challenges remain, including limited communication distances, noise in quantum channels, and the cost of implementation. Overcoming these hurdles will be essential for widespread adoption.

6.2 Drug Discovery and Material Science

Quantum computing has transformative potential in the fields of drug discovery and material science. These disciplines involve complex molecular interactions and systems that are computationally prohibitive to model using classical methods.

Molecular Simulation

Quantum computers excel at simulating quantum systems, including molecules. Unlike classical computers, which approximate molecular interactions, quantum computers can represent these interactions more accurately.

- **Drug Discovery:**
  Quantum simulations can accelerate the identification of promising drug candidates by accurately modeling how molecules interact with biological targets. For example:
  - **Protein Folding:** Quantum computers can predict protein structures more efficiently, aiding in the development of treatments for diseases like Alzheimer's and Parkinson's.
  - **Drug-Target Binding:** Quantum simulations can analyze how drugs bind to specific targets, optimizing efficacy and minimizing side effects.

- **Material Science:**
  In material science, quantum computing enables the discovery of new materials with desirable properties, such as superconductors, catalysts, and lightweight alloys. For example:
  - **Battery Technology:** Quantum simulations can improve energy storage materials, advancing battery technology for electric vehicles and renewable energy storage.

- **Catalyst Design:** Designing efficient catalysts for industrial processes can reduce costs and environmental impact.

Current Progress and Collaborations

Pharmaceutical giants like Pfizer and GlaxoSmithKline are collaborating with quantum computing companies to accelerate drug discovery. Similarly, material science researchers are leveraging quantum platforms to design innovative materials.

Challenges and Limitations

Despite its promise, quantum computing in this domain faces challenges such as:

- **Noisy Intermediate-Scale Quantum (NISQ) Systems:** Current quantum computers are noisy and lack the stability required for large-scale simulations.
- **Integration with Classical Methods:** Combining quantum simulations with classical computational methods remains complex.

6.3 Artificial Intelligence and Machine Learning

Artificial intelligence and machine learning are experiencing a paradigm shift with the advent of quantum computing. Quantum-enhanced algorithms can improve the speed and accuracy of various ML tasks, enabling breakthroughs in areas like natural language processing, image recognition, and predictive analytics.

Quantum Machine Learning (QML)

Quantum machine learning integrates quantum computing principles with traditional ML techniques.

- **Quantum Support Vector Machines (QSVM):**

  QSVMs leverage quantum feature spaces to classify data more efficiently than classical SVMs, especially in high-dimensional spaces.

- **Quantum Neural Networks (QNN):**

  QNNs mimic classical neural networks but operate on quantum data, enabling faster training and inference for complex datasets.

Applications of QML

- **Healthcare:**

  Quantum ML can improve diagnostic tools, personalize treatment plans, and analyze genetic data for precision medicine.

- **Finance:**

  Quantum-enhanced algorithms can optimize trading strategies, assess risk, and detect fraudulent activities.

- **Climate Modeling:**

  QML can enhance predictive models for climate change, helping policymakers devise effective mitigation strategies.

Optimization Problems

Many AI tasks involve optimization problems, such as minimizing loss functions in neural networks. Quantum computers excel at solving such problems using algorithms like the Quantum Approximate Optimization Algorithm (QAOA).

- **Logistics and Supply Chain Management:**

  Quantum optimization can streamline operations, reduce costs, and improve efficiency.

- **Robotics:**
  Quantum optimization aids in pathfinding and task planning for autonomous systems.

Challenges in Quantum AI/ML

- **Data Encoding:**
  Converting classical data into quantum states is a bottleneck for QML applications.

- **Noise and Error Rates:**
  Current quantum systems introduce errors that can compromise the accuracy of ML models.

- **Scalability:**
  Developing quantum hardware capable of handling large datasets is essential for realizing the full potential of QML.

Conclusion

The applications of quantum computing extend far beyond theoretical research, offering transformative solutions to real-world problems. In cryptography, quantum computers challenge traditional security methods while introducing new paradigms like QKD. In drug discovery and material science, quantum simulations hold the promise of accelerating innovation and reducing costs. Finally, in AI and ML, quantum algorithms offer the potential for unprecedented advances in data analysis and optimization.

Despite the challenges of noise, scalability, and integration, the rapid progress in quantum hardware and algorithm development is paving the way for practical applications. As quantum computing continues to mature, its impact on these fields will redefine the boundaries of what is computationally possible, ushering in a new era of technological innovation.

Chapter 7: Current Progress and Industry Leaders

Quantum computing has evolved from theoretical concepts to experimental breakthroughs, with significant milestones achieved in recent years. This progress is driven by academic research, corporate investment, and global competition, with technology giants and startups leading the charge. Chapter 7 delves into the milestones in quantum computing, highlights key industry players, and discusses the roadmap to quantum supremacy—a pivotal goal in the field.

7.1 Milestones in Quantum Computing

The journey of quantum computing has been marked by a series of theoretical and experimental breakthroughs that have steadily pushed the boundaries of possibility.

Theoretical Foundations

The concept of quantum computing was introduced in the 1980s by physicists such as Richard Feynman and David Deutsch. Feynman proposed using quantum systems to simulate physical processes, and Deutsch formalized the idea of a universal quantum computer. These foundations set the stage for further advancements.

Shor's Algorithm and Quantum Cryptography

In 1994, Peter Shor developed an algorithm for factoring large numbers exponentially faster than classical methods, demonstrating the potential of quantum computers to disrupt cryptography. Around the same time, the discovery of quantum key distribution (QKD) protocols like BB84 highlighted the security advantages of quantum systems.

Quantum Error Correction

In the mid-1990s, researchers like Peter Shor and Andrew Steane developed quantum error correction codes, addressing the challenge of noise and decoherence in quantum systems. This advancement was critical for making quantum computing practical.

Quantum Hardware Breakthroughs

- **2001:** IBM implemented Shor's algorithm on a 7-qubit system, a proof-of-concept demonstration of quantum computing's capabilities.

- **2011:** D-Wave Systems launched the first commercial quantum computer, though its focus on quantum annealing sparked debates about its classification as a "true" quantum computer.

Quantum Supremacy Milestone

In 2019, Google announced that its quantum processor, Sycamore, had achieved quantum supremacy. Sycamore completed a specific computation in 200 seconds that would take the world's fastest supercomputer thousands of years. While the milestone sparked debate over its practical implications, it underscored the rapid progress in quantum hardware.

Recent Achievements

- **2021:** IBM introduced the 127-qubit Eagle processor, marking a significant leap in qubit count and performance.

- **2022:** Researchers demonstrated advancements in quantum error correction, bringing fault-tolerant quantum computing closer to reality.

- **2023:** Hybrid quantum-classical approaches gained traction, leveraging the strengths of both systems to solve complex problems.

These milestones reflect the field's progression from theoretical exploration to tangible achievements that lay the groundwork for future innovations.

7.2 Key Players: IBM, Google, Microsoft, and Startups

The rapid development of quantum computing is fueled by a dynamic ecosystem of established tech giants, innovative startups, and academic institutions.

IBM

IBM is a pioneer in quantum computing, with its IBM Quantum program at the forefront of the industry.

- **Quantum Hardware:** IBM introduced processors like Falcon, Hummingbird, and Eagle, each increasing qubit count and coherence times.
- **Quantum Software:** IBM's Qiskit framework enables developers to write and execute quantum programs.
- **Quantum Network:** IBM Quantum Network connects academic and industrial partners, fostering collaboration and innovation.

IBM's focus on accessibility has made quantum computing more approachable, allowing researchers and businesses to experiment with quantum technologies.

Google

Google's quantum computing efforts are led by its Quantum AI division.

- **Quantum Supremacy:** Google's Sycamore processor was the first to achieve quantum supremacy in 2019.
- **Research Goals:** Google aims to develop a fault-tolerant quantum computer by the end of the decade.
- **Applications:** Google explores applications in optimization, AI, and scientific simulations.

Google's investments in quantum computing position it as a leader in both research and practical applications.

Microsoft

Microsoft takes a unique approach with its focus on topological qubits, which promise greater stability and error resistance.

- **Azure Quantum:** Microsoft's cloud-based quantum platform integrates tools like Q#, a quantum programming language.
- **Hybrid Systems:** Azure Quantum combines classical and quantum computing to tackle real-world problems.
- **Ecosystem:** Microsoft collaborates with hardware developers to offer diverse quantum systems on its platform.

Microsoft's emphasis on software and hybrid solutions aligns with its vision of integrating quantum computing into mainstream workflows.

Startups and Innovators

While tech giants dominate the quantum landscape, startups play a crucial role in driving innovation.

- **Rigetti Computing:** Known for its quantum cloud platform and emphasis on hybrid quantum-classical solutions.
- **IonQ:** Specializes in trapped-ion quantum computers, which offer high-fidelity qubits.
- **D-Wave Systems:** Focuses on quantum annealing for optimization problems.
- **Pasqal:** Explores neutral-atom quantum computing, a promising alternative to traditional approaches.

Startups often push the envelope by exploring niche technologies and addressing specific industry needs, complementing the broader efforts of established players.

7.3 The Roadmap to Quantum Supremacy

Achieving quantum supremacy—where a quantum computer outperforms classical computers on a practical task—is a pivotal goal for researchers and companies. However, the journey toward widespread quantum advantage involves overcoming significant challenges.

Scalability

Scaling quantum systems to thousands or millions of qubits is essential for practical applications. Current quantum computers are limited to a few hundred qubits, and adding more qubits introduces issues like noise and decoherence.

- **Modular Architectures:** Researchers are exploring modular designs that link smaller quantum processors into larger systems.
- **Error Correction:** Quantum error correction schemes are crucial for maintaining the fidelity of computations as systems scale.

Fault Tolerance

Fault-tolerant quantum computers can perform calculations reliably, even in the presence of errors. Achieving this requires:

- High-quality qubits with low error rates.
- Advanced error-correcting codes.
- Robust control systems to manage quantum states.

Hardware Innovations

Continued advancements in quantum hardware are necessary to improve performance and reduce costs. Promising technologies include:

- **Superconducting Qubits:** Widely used due to their scalability and compatibility with existing fabrication techniques.

- **Trapped Ions:** Known for their high coherence times and precision.

- **Photonic Quantum Computers:** Utilize light for fast and scalable quantum processing.

Software and Algorithms

Developing quantum software and algorithms is as important as improving hardware. Key areas of focus include:

- **Optimized Compilers:** Translating high-level quantum programs into efficient low-level instructions.

- **Algorithm Discovery:** Identifying new quantum algorithms for practical applications.

Global Collaboration and Competition

The race for quantum supremacy is a global endeavor, with countries like the U.S., China, and the EU investing heavily in quantum research. Collaborative initiatives and government funding programs play a vital role in advancing the field.

Ethical and Security Implications

As quantum computing approaches practicality, its societal implications must be addressed. These include:

- **Cryptographic Vulnerabilities:** Preparing for the transition to quantum-resistant cryptography.

- **Data Privacy:** Ensuring that quantum technologies are used responsibly.
- **Job Displacement:** Addressing workforce challenges as quantum computing automates complex tasks.

Conclusion

The progress in quantum computing is a testament to human ingenuity and perseverance. Milestones like the demonstration of Shor's algorithm, Google's quantum supremacy achievement, and IBM's advanced processors highlight how far the field has come. Industry leaders like IBM, Google, and Microsoft, alongside innovative startups, are shaping the future of quantum technology.

The roadmap to quantum supremacy is filled with challenges, from scaling hardware to ensuring fault tolerance. Yet, the collective efforts of researchers, companies, and governments are driving quantum computing toward practical applications that will revolutionize industries and redefine computation as we know it. With continued innovation and collaboration, the quantum future is not just possible—it is inevitable.

Chapter 8: Challenges and Ethical Considerations

Quantum computing, while promising transformative advancements across various fields, also presents significant challenges and ethical dilemmas. As this technology continues to evolve, addressing risks to data security and privacy, understanding its societal impacts, and grappling with complex ethical questions will be essential. This chapter explores the multifaceted challenges and ethical considerations that come with the rise of quantum computing.

8.1 Risks to Data Security and Privacy

One of the most immediate and well-documented concerns regarding quantum computing is its potential to undermine current data security frameworks. Modern cryptographic systems, which secure everything from online banking to government communications, rely on the difficulty of solving certain mathematical problems—challenges that quantum computers could potentially overcome.

The Vulnerability of Classical Cryptography

At the heart of modern digital security is public-key cryptography, which uses complex mathematical problems such as integer factorization (RSA) and discrete logarithms (Elliptic Curve Cryptography) to encrypt data. Classical computers struggle to solve these problems within a reasonable timeframe, making current encryption methods robust. However, quantum computers, equipped with algorithms like Shor's algorithm, can factorize large numbers exponentially faster than classical computers.

This capability creates a critical vulnerability. If a sufficiently powerful quantum computer were developed, encrypted communications could be decrypted, exposing sensitive information. Industries that rely heavily on secure communications, including finance, healthcare, and national security, are at risk.

Quantum-Resistant Cryptography

In response to these threats, researchers are developing post-quantum cryptographic algorithms designed to withstand attacks from both classical and quantum computers. These algorithms rely on mathematical problems that are hard for quantum computers to solve, such as lattice-based cryptography and multivariate polynomial equations. The National Institute of Standards and Technology (NIST) has been actively evaluating potential quantum-resistant algorithms, signaling the urgency of this transition.

The Risk of Quantum Attacks Today

Even though large-scale quantum computers do not yet exist, the risk of "harvest now, decrypt later" attacks is real. Malicious actors can store encrypted data today, with the intention of decrypting it once quantum computers become capable. This raises immediate concerns for industries managing long-term sensitive information, such as healthcare records, legal contracts, and government data.

Ethical Dilemmas in Data Privacy

Quantum computing challenges the traditional understanding of data privacy. Questions arise about who should control access to quantum capabilities, how vulnerabilities in encryption will be addressed, and whether governments or private entities will exploit these advancements for surveillance or other questionable practices.

8.2 Societal Impacts of Quantum Technologies

Quantum computing has the potential to reshape society in profound ways, but these changes may not benefit everyone equally. As with any transformative technology, quantum computing introduces risks of inequity, disruption, and unintended consequences.

Economic Disruption and Workforce Challenges

Quantum computing will revolutionize industries such as finance, healthcare, logistics, and artificial intelligence. However, this revolution may also displace workers, as automation and optimization reduce the need for certain roles. While new jobs will undoubtedly emerge, they will likely require specialized training and skills in quantum programming, hardware development, and algorithm design.

For countries or communities that lack access to quantum education or infrastructure, the economic gap may widen, leading to greater global inequality. Ensuring equitable access to quantum technology and its benefits will be a key challenge for policymakers and industry leaders.

Global Competition and Geopolitical Tensions

Quantum computing is at the center of a global race for technological dominance. Countries like the United States, China, and members of the European Union are investing billions in quantum research and development.

While healthy competition can drive innovation, it can also lead to geopolitical tensions. The fear of falling behind in quantum capabilities may push nations to prioritize quantum computing for military applications, intelligence gathering, and economic leverage. These dynamics could exacerbate international conflicts and undermine efforts to use quantum technology for the common good.

Impact on Developing Nations

While technologically advanced nations lead quantum research, developing countries risk being left behind. If quantum computing becomes a tool for solving critical problems such as climate modeling or resource optimization, access to this technology will be crucial. Bridging the digital divide and ensuring that developing nations can participate in the quantum revolution will be vital for fostering global equity.

8.3 Ethical Questions in Quantum Computing

The ethical implications of quantum computing go beyond its technical challenges. As with any disruptive technology, its development and application raise questions about fairness, accountability, and moral responsibility.

Who Controls Quantum Computing?

One of the most fundamental ethical dilemmas is the issue of control. Should quantum computing be the domain of private corporations, governments, or international organizations?

- **Corporate Dominance:** Technology giants such as IBM, Google, and Microsoft are leading the development of quantum computers. While their contributions drive innovation, corporate control raises concerns about monopolization and profit-driven decision-making at the expense of public benefit.

- **Government Oversight:** Governments could regulate quantum computing to ensure its ethical use, but this may lead to surveillance, misuse, or restricted access for certain groups.

- **Global Governance:** An international body overseeing quantum technology could promote equitable access and ethical guidelines, but such a system would require unprecedented levels of cooperation and trust among nations.

The Ethical Use of Quantum Power

Quantum computing's immense computational power can be both a blessing and a curse. While it has the potential to solve pressing global problems, it could also be misused for harmful purposes. For example:

- **Positive Applications:** Quantum computing could accelerate drug discovery, optimize renewable energy systems, and improve climate models.
- **Negative Applications:** The same power could be used to develop more sophisticated cyberattacks, invasive surveillance systems, or even autonomous weapons.

Ethical guidelines will be necessary to ensure that quantum computing is used responsibly. Researchers and developers must adopt principles of transparency, accountability, and fairness as they advance the technology.

Privacy in a Post-Quantum World

Quantum computing's ability to crack encryption raises deeper philosophical questions about privacy. If data is no longer secure, what safeguards can society implement to protect individual rights? Will governments or corporations have the moral authority to use quantum decryption for law enforcement or national security purposes?

Moral Responsibility of Researchers

Scientists and engineers working on quantum computing bear a significant ethical responsibility. They must consider the societal implications of their work, anticipate potential misuse, and advocate for safeguards to prevent harm. This responsibility extends to:

- Designing secure quantum systems.

- Participating in public dialogue about quantum ethics.
- Educating policymakers and the public about the technology's risks and benefits.

Quantum Ethics Frameworks

To address these questions, scholars and ethicists are beginning to propose frameworks for quantum ethics. These frameworks draw on principles from AI ethics, bioethics, and cybersecurity, emphasizing the need for:

- **Inclusivity:** Ensuring diverse voices are included in decision-making.
- **Sustainability:** Considering the environmental impact of quantum hardware and operations.
- **Equitability:** Promoting access to quantum technology across different socioeconomic and geographic groups.

Conclusion

Quantum computing represents a paradigm shift in technology, offering unprecedented opportunities and equally significant challenges. The risks to data security and privacy are immediate and far-reaching, requiring proactive measures to transition to quantum-resistant encryption. The societal impacts of quantum technologies, from economic disruption to global inequality, underscore the need for careful planning and equitable policies.

Ethical questions surrounding control, use, and access to quantum computing demand thoughtful deliberation. Whether quantum technology becomes a tool for global progress or a source of division depends on how society navigates these challenges. By addressing these considerations now, researchers, policymakers, and industry leaders can ensure that the quantum future is as ethical as it is transformative.

Chapter 9: The Future of Quantum Computing

Quantum computing stands at the frontier of technological innovation, promising breakthroughs in solving problems that classical computers struggle to address. As the field progresses, its influence will expand across industries, economies, and societies. This chapter explores what the future might hold for quantum computing, including predictions for the next two decades, its integration with classical computing, and its potential role in addressing global challenges.

9.1 Predictions for the Next Two Decades

The trajectory of quantum computing is marked by rapid advancements in hardware, software, and theoretical research. Experts anticipate significant milestones in the next 20 years, transforming the landscape of computing and society as a whole.

The Road to Fault-Tolerant Quantum Computing

Currently, quantum computers are in the *noisy intermediate-scale quantum (NISQ)* era, where quantum systems are prone to errors and limited in scalability. Over the next two decades, researchers aim to achieve *fault-tolerant quantum computing*, where error correction mechanisms enable long and reliable computations. Fault tolerance is the key to unlocking the full potential of quantum systems, paving the way for more robust applications in cryptography, chemistry, and artificial intelligence.

Commercial Quantum Applications

As quantum computers become more powerful and reliable, they will transition from research labs to commercial use. Industries such as finance, pharmaceuticals, and logistics will adopt quantum computing to optimize operations, develop innovative products, and gain a competitive edge. For instance:

- **Finance:** Quantum computers will revolutionize risk analysis, portfolio optimization, and fraud detection.

- **Healthcare:** Quantum simulations will accelerate drug discovery and personalized medicine.

- **Energy:** Advanced algorithms will optimize renewable energy grids and improve battery technologies.

Quantum Supremacy and Beyond

Quantum supremacy—the point at which a quantum computer can solve a problem no classical computer can—was achieved by Google in 2019 for a specific computational task. Over the next two decades, quantum systems are expected to surpass classical capabilities in solving real-world problems, achieving what some call *quantum advantage*. This milestone will mark the beginning of quantum computing's widespread impact across various fields.

Global Quantum Networks

Another exciting prediction involves the rise of quantum networks, where quantum computers are interconnected to share and process information. Quantum networks, powered by quantum entanglement and teleportation, could lead to the development of a *quantum internet*. Such a network would provide ultra-secure communication, faster data transmission, and distributed quantum computing capabilities.

9.2 Integration of Quantum and Classical Computing

While quantum computers are poised to outperform classical systems in certain areas, they will not replace classical computing. Instead, the future of computing lies in the integration of quantum and classical systems, where each complements the other's strengths.

Hybrid Computing Models

Hybrid quantum-classical systems will emerge as the standard approach to leveraging quantum power. In such models:

- Classical computers handle pre-processing and post-processing tasks, such as data input, visualization, and result interpretation.

- Quantum computers perform the computationally intensive quantum operations, such as solving optimization problems or simulating quantum systems.

For example, in machine learning, a hybrid system might use classical algorithms to prepare datasets and quantum algorithms to optimize neural networks. This collaboration allows for practical applications of quantum computing without requiring it to operate independently.

Middleware and Software Platforms

The integration of quantum and classical systems will require middleware and advanced software platforms to bridge the gap. Companies like IBM, Google, and Microsoft are already developing cloud-based platforms where users can access quantum processors alongside classical ones. These platforms enable developers to write programs that seamlessly combine quantum and classical code, accelerating adoption across industries.

Interdisciplinary Collaboration

The integration of quantum and classical systems will also foster interdisciplinary collaboration. Quantum computing's applications in fields like biology, cryptography, and economics will require experts from diverse disciplines to work together. For instance, a team solving climate modeling might include quantum physicists, climate scientists, and software engineers.

9.3 Quantum Computing's Role in Global Challenges

Quantum computing holds immense potential for addressing some of the world's most pressing challenges. From combating climate change to enhancing global security, this technology could play a pivotal role in shaping a sustainable and equitable future.

Combating Climate Change

Quantum computing could revolutionize our understanding of climate systems and help mitigate the effects of climate change. Potential applications include:

- **Climate Modeling:** Quantum systems can simulate complex interactions in the Earth's climate, providing more accurate predictions of weather patterns and long-term climate changes.

- **Energy Optimization:** Quantum algorithms can improve the efficiency of renewable energy sources, optimize energy grids, and enhance battery storage technologies.

- **Carbon Capture:** Quantum chemistry simulations could lead to breakthroughs in carbon capture and storage methods, reducing greenhouse gas emissions.

Advancing Healthcare and Medicine

The healthcare industry stands to benefit enormously from quantum computing, particularly in drug discovery and personalized medicine:

- **Drug Discovery:** Quantum computers can simulate molecular interactions at an unprecedented scale, speeding up the development of new drugs and reducing costs.

- **Genomics:** Quantum algorithms could process vast genomic datasets, enabling more effective treatments tailored to individual patients.

- **Epidemiology:** Quantum-powered simulations can model the spread of diseases and optimize strategies for containment and vaccination.

Enhancing Global Security

Quantum computing will redefine the landscape of cybersecurity and national security:

- **Quantum-Resistant Encryption:** As quantum computers threaten classical encryption, developing quantum-resistant cryptographic methods will be crucial to ensuring secure communication.

- **Secure Communications:** Quantum key distribution (QKD) provides ultra-secure communication channels, immune to eavesdropping.

- **Defense Applications:** Quantum simulations could optimize defense strategies, logistics, and decision-making in complex scenarios.

Addressing Food and Water Scarcity

Quantum computing could also contribute to solving global issues of food and water scarcity:

- **Agricultural Optimization:** Quantum algorithms can analyze variables such as weather patterns, soil conditions, and crop genetics to maximize agricultural yields.

- **Water Resource Management:** Quantum simulations could optimize the distribution and purification of water resources, reducing waste and ensuring equitable access.

Ethical and Equitable Development

As quantum computing addresses global challenges, ensuring ethical and equitable development will be vital. This includes:

- Ensuring access to quantum technologies for developing nations.

- Preventing misuse of quantum power for surveillance or warfare.

- Balancing innovation with environmental sustainability, given the energy-intensive nature of quantum hardware.

Conclusion

The future of quantum computing is both exhilarating and complex. Over the next two decades, advancements in fault tolerance, hybrid computing, and quantum networks will unlock transformative applications across industries. The integration of quantum and classical computing will create a harmonious ecosystem where the strengths of both systems are leveraged to solve real-world problems.

Quantum computing's potential to address global challenges—from climate change to healthcare and security—positions it as a cornerstone of technological progress. However, realizing this potential will require collaboration across disciplines, careful ethical considerations, and a commitment to equitable development.

As quantum computing continues to evolve, it will redefine our understanding of what is computationally possible, ushering in an era of unprecedented innovation and opportunity. The journey ahead is as much about technological breakthroughs as it is about ensuring these advancements benefit humanity as a whole.

Chapter 10: Glossary of Quantum Computing Terms

This glossary provides a comprehensive list of key terms and concepts in quantum computing. Whether you're a beginner or an advanced learner, this section will serve as a quick reference to better understand the technical language used throughout this book.

Algorithm

A set of step-by-step instructions designed to perform a specific task or solve a problem. In quantum computing, algorithms like Shor's and Grover's utilize quantum mechanics to achieve tasks faster than classical algorithms.

Amplitude

The complex number associated with the probability of a quantum state. The square of the amplitude gives the probability of observing that state when measured.

Bell State

A specific quantum state of two qubits that are maximally entangled. Bell states demonstrate the phenomenon of quantum entanglement and are fundamental to quantum communication protocols.

Bit

The basic unit of information in classical computing, represented as either 0 or 1.

Bloch Sphere

A geometric representation of a single qubit's state. Points on the surface of the sphere represent all possible pure quantum states of the qubit.

Classical Computing

The traditional model of computing based on bits, logic gates, and deterministic operations.

Clifford Gates

A subset of quantum gates used in quantum error correction and stabilizer codes. Examples include the Hadamard gate and the Pauli-X gate.

Coherence

The property of a quantum system that allows superposition and interference to occur. Loss of coherence, or decoherence, leads to errors in quantum computations.

Cryptography

The practice of secure communication through encoding and decoding information. Quantum computing has implications for both breaking existing cryptographic systems and creating new, secure protocols.

Decoherence

The process by which a quantum system loses its quantum properties due to interaction with its environment, effectively turning quantum behavior into classical behavior.

Entanglement

A quantum phenomenon where the states of two or more particles become linked such that the state of one instantly determines the state of the other, no matter the distance between them.

Error Correction

Techniques used to detect and correct errors in quantum computations caused by noise, decoherence, and other quantum imperfections. Quantum error correction is critical for fault-tolerant quantum computing.

Gate

An operation performed on qubits to change their state. Quantum gates, such as the Hadamard gate and the CNOT gate, manipulate quantum states and are the building blocks of quantum circuits.

Grover's Algorithm

A quantum algorithm used for searching an unsorted database with N entries in $O(\sqrt{N})$ time, offering a quadratic speedup over classical search methods.

Hadamard Gate (H-Gate)

A quantum gate that creates a superposition state from a classical state (0 or 1). It is often used to initialize qubits in a quantum circuit.

Hybrid Computing

A computing paradigm that combines quantum and classical computing resources to solve complex problems efficiently.

Interference

The phenomenon in quantum mechanics where wave-like quantum states combine, leading to constructive or destructive patterns that affect probabilities in quantum computations.

Noisy Intermediate-Scale Quantum (NISQ)

The current era of quantum computing, characterized by devices with limited qubits and error rates that make them unsuitable for large-scale fault-tolerant computations.

Oracle

A black-box function used in quantum algorithms like Grover's to encode a problem into a quantum circuit for solving.

Pauli Gates

A set of single-qubit quantum gates named after physicist Wolfgang Pauli. They include the Pauli-X (NOT), Pauli-Y, and Pauli-Z gates, which perform specific transformations on qubits.

Post-Quantum Cryptography

A field of cryptography that develops encryption methods resistant to attacks by quantum computers, ensuring data security in a quantum-enabled world.

Probability Amplitude

The complex number associated with the likelihood of a quantum state being observed.

Qubit (Quantum Bit)

The fundamental unit of quantum information, analogous to a classical bit but capable of representing 0, 1, or any quantum superposition of these states.

Quantum Circuit

A sequence of quantum gates applied to qubits to perform a computation. Quantum circuits are the quantum equivalent of classical algorithms.

Quantum Entanglement

A phenomenon where the quantum states of two or more particles become interconnected, such that the measurement of one particle instantly determines the state of the others.

Quantum Gate

An operation on qubits that changes their quantum states. Gates are the building blocks of quantum algorithms and can manipulate superposition, entanglement, and other quantum properties.

Quantum Key Distribution (QKD)

A secure communication method that uses quantum mechanics to encrypt and transmit keys for secure communication.

Quantum Mechanics

The fundamental theory of physics that describes the behavior of matter and energy at the quantum scale, forming the basis of quantum computing.

Quantum Supremacy

The milestone where a quantum computer performs a computation that is infeasible for a classical computer to solve within a reasonable timeframe.

Quantum Tunneling

A phenomenon where particles pass through a barrier that they classically shouldn't be able to cross, often used in quantum hardware design.

Quantum Volume

A metric that evaluates the performance of a quantum computer, considering factors like qubit count, error rates, and connectivity.

Quantum Algorithm

A set of instructions designed to run on a quantum computer, leveraging quantum mechanics to solve problems more efficiently than classical algorithms.

Quantum Annealing

A quantum computing approach optimized for solving optimization problems by finding the lowest-energy configuration of a system.

Quantum Computer

A machine that uses the principles of quantum mechanics to perform computations, leveraging phenomena like superposition, entanglement, and interference.

Quantum Cryptography

A field of study focused on creating cryptographic methods that leverage quantum mechanics to enhance security, such as quantum key distribution.

Quantum Decoherence

The loss of quantum coherence in a system due to interaction with the environment, leading to errors in quantum computations.

Quantum Supremacy

The point where a quantum computer performs a task beyond the capabilities of the most powerful classical computers.

Shor's Algorithm

A quantum algorithm that efficiently factors large integers, posing a threat to traditional encryption systems like RSA.

Superposition

A fundamental principle of quantum mechanics where a quantum system exists simultaneously in multiple states until measured.

Tensor Product

A mathematical operation used to describe the combined states of multiple quantum systems.

Teleportation (Quantum)

The transfer of quantum information (like a qubit's state) from one location to another without physically transmitting the particle itself, using entanglement.

Universal Quantum Computer

A theoretical quantum computer that can perform any computation, similar to a classical Turing machine.

Wavefunction

A mathematical function describing the quantum state of a system. The square of its magnitude gives the probability of finding the system in a particular state.

This glossary encapsulates the essential terms and concepts of quantum computing, equipping you with the foundational language to navigate this rapidly evolving field. For more in-depth explanations, consult the resources listed in Chapter 11.

Further Resources

The journey to understanding quantum computing doesn't end with this book. The field is evolving rapidly, with new breakthroughs and developments occurring regularly. This chapter provides a curated list of further resources—books, online courses, and communities—to deepen your knowledge and stay updated on the latest advancements.

11.1 Recommended Books

1. *Quantum Computing for Everyone* by Chris Bernhardt

A beginner-friendly introduction to the principles of quantum computing. This book simplifies complex concepts, making them accessible to readers without a technical background.

2. *Quantum Computation and Quantum Information* by Michael A. Nielsen and Isaac L. Chuang

Known as the "bible" of quantum computing, this book is a comprehensive and rigorous resource for those seeking an in-depth understanding of the field.

3. *An Introduction to Quantum Computing* by Phillip Kaye, Raymond Laflamme, and Michele Mosca

A concise and practical guide to quantum computing, focusing on its mathematical foundations and algorithms like Shor's and Grover's.

4. *Quantum Mechanics and Path Integrals* by Richard P. Feynman and Albert R. Hibbs

A classic text on quantum mechanics that provides foundational knowledge relevant to understanding quantum computing.

5. *The Feynman Lectures on Physics: Volume 3* by **Richard P. Feynman, Robert B. Leighton, and Matthew Sands**

This volume of the famous lecture series covers quantum mechanics in a clear and engaging style, suitable for those looking to build a deeper theoretical foundation.

6. *Qiskit Textbook: Learn Quantum Computing with Python and Qiskit*

An open-source book developed by IBM, specifically designed to teach quantum computing programming using the Qiskit framework.

11.2 Online Courses and Tutorials

1. *Introduction to Quantum Computing* **by IBM (edX)**

A free course designed for beginners, covering the basics of quantum mechanics, quantum circuits, and programming with Qiskit.

2. *Quantum Mechanics for Scientists and Engineers* **by Stanford University (edX)**

A comprehensive course that bridges quantum mechanics and its applications, ideal for building the theoretical background needed for quantum computing.

3. *Quantum Computing for Everyone* **by MIT (edX)**

An excellent starting point for non-experts, this course introduces quantum computing concepts and applications.

4. *The Qiskit Global Summer School* **(IBM Quantum)**

An annual program that offers intensive quantum computing training, focusing on quantum circuits, algorithms, and practical implementation using Qiskit.

5. *Quantum Computing Specialization* by University of Toronto (Coursera)

A series of courses that delve into quantum computing fundamentals, algorithms, and practical applications.

6. *Quantum Programming Tutorials* on YouTube

Channels like *Qiskit* and *Quantum Country* offer short, practical tutorials for programming quantum computers.

7. *Microsoft Learn: Quantum Computing* (Microsoft)

A series of modules focusing on quantum development using Microsoft's Quantum Development Kit and Q#.

11.3 Quantum Computing Communities

1. IBM Quantum Experience

An online platform that provides access to real quantum computers and simulators. It includes an active community forum where users can discuss problems, share projects, and collaborate.

Website: IBM Quantum Experience

2. Qiskit Community

A global community of quantum computing enthusiasts and developers who use IBM's Qiskit framework. The community organizes events, hackathons, and workshops.

Website: Qiskit Community

3. Stack Exchange: Quantum Computing

A dedicated section on Stack Exchange where users can ask and answer questions related to quantum computing, from basic concepts to advanced programming challenges.

Website: Quantum Computing Stack Exchange

4. Quantum Open Source Foundation (QOSF)

An organization promoting open-source projects in quantum computing. It offers mentorship programs, project collaborations, and a welcoming space for newcomers.

Website: QOSF

5. Reddit: r/QuantumComputing

A lively subreddit where enthusiasts and experts share news, tutorials, and discussions about quantum computing developments.

Website: r/QuantumComputing

6. LinkedIn Groups

Professional networking groups like "Quantum Computing Enthusiasts" and "Quantum Computing and Quantum Information Science" provide platforms for discussions, job opportunities, and staying informed about industry trends.

7. Meetup Groups

Search for local or virtual quantum computing meetups to network with others interested in the field. Events often feature talks by experts and opportunities to collaborate.

Conclusion

This curated list of resources ensures that you can expand your knowledge and engage with the vibrant quantum computing ecosystem. Whether you prefer reading, hands-on programming, or collaborative learning, there's a resource here to suit your needs.

By exploring these books, courses, and communities, you'll be well-equipped to navigate the exciting journey of quantum computing and stay ahead in this transformative field.

References

This chapter lists the key sources referenced throughout the book. These materials have been carefully selected to ensure the accuracy and depth of information on quantum computing. Whether you are seeking foundational knowledge or in-depth technical details, the following resources provide valuable insights.

Books

1. Bernhardt, Chris. *Quantum Computing for Everyone.* MIT Press, 2019.

2. Nielsen, Michael A., and Isaac L. Chuang. *Quantum Computation and Quantum Information.* Cambridge University Press, 2010.

3. Kaye, Phillip, Raymond Laflamme, and Michele Mosca. *An Introduction to Quantum Computing.* Oxford University Press, 2007.

4. Feynman, Richard P., and Albert R. Hibbs. *Quantum Mechanics and Path Integrals.* Dover Publications, 2010.

5. Preskill, John. *Lecture Notes on Quantum Computation.* California Institute of Technology, 1998.

6. Barenco, Adriano. "Quantum Gates: A Review." *Progress in Physics of Quantum Computation,* 1995.

Research Papers

1. Shor, Peter W. "Algorithms for Quantum Computation: Discrete Logarithms and Factoring." *Proceedings of the 35th Annual Symposium on Foundations of Computer Science*, 1994.

2. Grover, Lov K. "A Fast Quantum Mechanical Algorithm for Database Search." *Proceedings of the 28th Annual ACM Symposium on Theory of Computing*, 1996.

3. Deutsch, David. "Quantum Theory, the Church-Turing Principle, and the Universal Quantum Computer." *Proceedings of the Royal Society of London. A. Mathematical and Physical Sciences*, 1985.

Websites and Online Resources

1. IBM Quantum. "What is Quantum Computing?" IBM Quantum Website, 2024.

   https://quantum-computing.ibm.com/

2. Microsoft Quantum Development Kit. "Quantum Computing with Q#," Microsoft Learn, 2024.

   https://learn.microsoft.com/en-us/azure/quantum/

3. Qiskit. "Quantum Programming Tutorials," Qiskit Website, 2024.

   https://qiskit.org/

4. Quantum Open Source Foundation (QOSF). "Mentorship Program and Open-Source Projects," QOSF, 2024.

   https://qosf.org/

Articles and Blog Posts

1. Aaronson, Scott. "The Limits of Quantum Computers." *Scientific American*, 2008.

2. Monroe, Christopher. "The Future of Quantum Computing: Challenges and Opportunities." *Nature Physics,* 2021.

3. Knight, Will. "Google Claims Quantum Supremacy." *MIT Technology Review,* October 2019.

Courses and Tutorials

1. Stanford University. "Quantum Mechanics for Scientists and Engineers," edX, 2024.

    https://online.stanford.edu/courses/

2. MIT. "Quantum Computing for Everyone," edX, 2024.

    https://edx.org/course/quantum-computing-for-everyone

Key Institutions and Publications

1. IBM Research. *Quantum Volume Reports*, 2024.

2. Google Quantum AI. *Milestones in Quantum Supremacy*, 2024.

3. European Quantum Flagship. "Quantum Computing Progress in Europe." *Official Reports,* 2023.

Acknowledgements

These references have provided the foundational material for creating a comprehensive overview of quantum computing. The contributions from researchers, authors, and institutions have made it possible to explain complex topics in an accessible way. For readers eager to delve deeper into any specific topic, these sources offer an excellent starting point.

Author's Note

Writing this book has been a journey of exploration into one of the most fascinating frontiers of modern science: quantum computing. As an author, my aim was to demystify the complexities of this revolutionary field and make it accessible to readers with varying levels of technical expertise. Whether you're a curious novice, a tech enthusiast, or a seasoned professional, I hope this book has provided you with valuable insights into the world of quantum computing.

Quantum computing stands at the intersection of science, technology, and philosophy. It challenges our fundamental understanding of computation and pushes the boundaries of what is possible. As someone deeply intrigued by both the technical and societal implications of quantum technologies, I felt compelled to write a book that not only explains the science but also sparks conversations about the broader impacts of this transformative technology.

This book would not have been possible without the inspiration and contributions of many individuals and communities. Quantum computing is a rapidly evolving field, and the wealth of knowledge shared by researchers, developers, and educators worldwide is a testament to the collaborative spirit that drives scientific progress. I am immensely grateful to those who have dedicated their lives to advancing this technology and making their findings accessible to the broader public.

I also recognize that, despite the advancements outlined in this book, quantum computing is still in its infancy. Many of the breakthroughs discussed here are milestones on a much longer road. The journey ahead will undoubtedly bring challenges, but it will also bring unprecedented opportunities to address global problems and improve the human condition.

As you finish reading this book, I encourage you to stay curious and engaged. Whether by exploring the recommended resources, joining quantum computing communities, or simply keeping an open mind to the possibilities of this technology, your interest is part of what fuels the progress of science.

Lastly, a personal note: writing about quantum computing has reminded me of the profound beauty of the universe's mysteries. It is humbling to contemplate how quantum mechanics underpins so much of our reality, from the smallest particles to the grandest innovations. In understanding quantum computing, we not only unlock new computational power but also deepen our connection to the fundamental fabric of existence.

Thank you for joining me on this journey. I hope this book has inspired you to learn, question, and dream about the quantum future that lies ahead.

With gratitude and excitement,

Oluchi Ike

www.ingramcontent.com/pod-product-compliance
Lightning Source LLC
Chambersburg PA
CBHW082252220526
45469CB00009B/2975